D0914210

JUNIOR HIGH JOURNALISM

By
HOMER L. HALL

THE ROSEN PUBLISHING GROUP
New York

Published in 1969, 1972, 1976, 1978, 1981, 1984 by
The Rosen Publishing Group, Inc.
29 East 21st Street, New York City, N.Y. 10010

Revised Edition 1984

Library of Congress Cataloging in Publication Data

Hall, Homer L
   Junior high journalism.

   Bibliography: p.
   Includes index.
   1. Journalism, Junior high school.   I.   Title.
LB3621.4.H34   1980   373.18'97   76–8193
ISBN 0–8239–0370–2

Manufactured in the United States of America

TABLE OF CONTENTS

HOMER HALL, yearbook and newspaper sponsor at Kirkwood High School, Kirkwood, Missouri, has devoted much of his working life to scholastic journalism. Before going to Kirkwood High School in 1973, he sponsored a senior high newspaper for one year at Shawnee-Mission East High School, Shawnee-Mission, Kansas, and a junior high newspaper and yearbook for eight years at North Kirkwood Junior High.

During his time at Shawnee-Mission East, the school newspaper received its first All-American rating from the National Scholastic Press Association.

At North Kirkwood Junior High he instituted a monthly printed newspaper, instead of the previous mimeographed sheet. Members of his junior high class won several honors, including first place on five occasions in a junior high writing contest in the St. Louis area and first place in a statewide junior and senior high Newspaper Week contest. The junior high paper was rated Medalist by the Columbia Scholastic Press Association and All-Missouri by the Missouri Interscholastic Press Association.

The Kirkwood High paper has been rated Medalist, All-American, and All-Missouri and has received the George H. Gallup Award from Quill & Scroll. The yearbook has been rated All-American, Medalist, and All-Missouri. In 1982 the newspaper was named an NSPA regional Pacemaker winner, and the yearbook was one of five senior high books in the country to receive the Pacemaker Award. It also received CSPA's Gold Crown Award given to the top 1 percent of the books in the country.

Growing up on a farm near Avilla, Missouri, Hall spent his early school years in a one-room schoolhouse. He attended high school at Carthage and won a Curator's scholarship to the University of Missouri. There he earned a B.S. degree in education, and he received an M.S. degree from the University of Kansas.

His interest in journalism was furthered by his two years in military service, during which he served as a lieutenant and was public information officer and editor of the *Hercules Herald* for the 1st Missile Battalion, 62nd Artillery, at Scott Air Force Base, Illinois.

In 1965 he was awarded a fellowship by the *Wall Street Journal* to attend a Newspaper Fund Seminar at the University of Minnesota. For two consecutive years (1966–67) he received $150 awards from the Newspaper Fund for his work as a journalism teacher. In 1968 he was named runner-up teacher of the year by the Fund and was presented with a $500 award (highest ever given to a junior high teacher).

In 1973 he was named Missouri Journalism Teacher of the Year, and in 1975 he was awarded the Medal of Merit by the Journalism Education Association for his contributions to the field of journalism. In 1979 he was named Missouri Teacher of the Year, and in 1982 he received the NSPA Pioneer Award, the CSPA Gold Key Award, the MIPA Taft Award, and the Newspaper Fund's National Journalism Teacher of the Year Award.

He is a contributing editor for *Communication: Journalism Education Today*, a publication of the Journalism Education Association, and has served as president of the Missouri Journalism Education Association, as president of the Sponsors of School Publications of Greater St. Louis, as a JEA state director, and as a member of the JEA junior high curriculum commission.

Other journalism experience includes serving as a reporter for the Sedalia *Democrat*, Sedalia, Missouri, and as Publicity Director of the Sedalia Public Schools.

PREFACE

Junior High Journalism was designed to meet the basic needs of the average junior-high student. The book will not answer questions to all problems that might arise but will serve as a guideline as to how to solve most situations.

Junior High Journalism is intended to aid junior high newspaper and yearbook staff members in writing and editing situations. As such, it does not cover the areas of production, circulation, and financing.

What better place is there to begin writing in a clear, concise style, than right now—in junior high? Fragment sentences, jumbled paragraphs, and bumpy transitions are all hurdles you've managed to clear. Here is the chance to get the jump on journalistic writing. At the same time, you'll master the jargon and various techniques of journalism. The field of journalism has an ever-expanding horizon. Even in this first acquaintance with it, you'll find journalism broadening and enriching your own personality.

Publication of *Junior High Journalism* was made possible by Patrick Kennedy and Paul Swensson, former assistant director and executive director respectively of The Newspaper Fund, Inc. Their interest and support were most encouraging. Acknowledgment is also given to those junior high schools who gave permission to reprint articles from their papers or spreads from their yearbooks. Thanks are also given to Professor George Hage of the University of Minnesota and to Evelyn Cassidy, Lori Pierce, Steve Steinberg, Hilda Walker, Jerry Newell, and Susan Wright, junior high advisers, who provided examples for this 1983 revision. Their cooperation, along with other advisers who provided examples that remain from earlier editions, help make this book possible. A special thanks also to my wife, Lea Ann, and my daughters, Lynlea and Ashley.

Chapter I

INTRODUCTION

When Johann Gutenberg invented movable type in 1454, the world received perhaps its greatest invention.

Before his invention, man's written communication was limited. The ancient Babylonians used a stone wedge to gouge messages in blocks of clay. It was not too complicated, and most people easily mastered the letter system; however, the clay tablets wore out very quickly.

The Egyptians developed a system of hieroglyphics that was quite advanced for their era, but it proved to be too cumbersome and complicated for the ordinary person to use.

In the Europe of Gutenberg's day, written communication was left mostly to scientists, monks, philosophers, and noblemen. Few books were written. Writing a book by hand was a long and laborious process. Monks spent an entire lifetime on one book, writing with meticulous care and sometimes adding elaborate gold decorations. Even these few books were written in Latin, and therefore, the people of Germany, Britain, and other European countries were limited in means to learn about the rest of the world.

In A.D. 770 the Chinese invented wood-block printing, carving characters on wooden blocks by hand. Pi Sheng was actually the first to use movable type. His system was very cumbersome, however, since the Chinese language contained more than 1,000 letters and characters. The wood-block system was used until Western civilization began to wield its influence in the Orient.

During the Middle Ages, little progress was made toward cultural improvement. In Italy in the fifteenth century, however, some men began to further the cause of culture, giving rise to the Renaissance. More and more people took up the cause. People began to appreciate the world around them. And why? Because of Gutenberg's historic invention. With printing so simplified, books were less of a rarity. The ancient legends and myths that had been handed on by word of mouth for centuries could be set down on paper for all the peoples of the world to read. The Bible, the greatest of all books, became available to everyone. Discoveries, inventions, and conquests could be recorded for future ages.

Today it is clear how greatly printing has contributed to our civilization. Education, for instance, has come a long way since the fifteenth century. Books and newspapers play an important role in education by bringing the world closer to the student.

Printing has led to many improvements. The Wright Brothers got their idea for the airplane from a printed book. The Montgolfiers got the idea for a balloon from something they read. Printing of books led to printing of newspapers, magazines, and other material.

The printed word did much to develop our American freedom. A man named Thomas Paine wrote a pamphlet called "Common Sense" that aroused a continent. Alexander Hamilton, John Jay, and James Madison wrote a series of articles called "The Federalist Papers," which helped a struggling nation to form a Constitution. A young woman named Harriet Beecher Stowe wrote a book, *Uncle Tom's Cabin,* that was a significant factor in the events leading to the Civil War and caused President Abraham Lincoln to say to her, "So you are the little lady that started all this!"

Printing is one of the most essential industries in modern life. Without it, we would have only a few handwritten books and no calendars, postage stamps, newspapers, paper money, or other important products.

Education is based on printing. Printing has made books and famous documents available to school children throughout the world. Students learn about government, history, science, mathematics, and many other subjects from printed books.

Uneducated, superstitious people in Asia, Africa, and parts of the United States have been helped to fight their illiteracy and ignorance by the millions of copies of books that are being printed each day. Almost everyone in the United States can now read and write, whereas in the olden days, when few books were printed or available, hardly anyone was literate.

People die and buildings crumble, but books live on, immortalizing the works of men. Books tell of dragons and knights and castles. They tell of struggles for power, of assassinations, and of coronations. They tell of the ocean, the earth, and space; and they tell of God and Satan. Without books part of every man would die. A book can be a magic carpet into never-never land, where the world is the way we would like it to be, or a door to new intellectual horizons.

Printing has also promoted business through the use of advertising. The more than 10,000,000 businesses in the United States spend almost $100,000,000 annually on advertising. Newspaper advertising accounts for about $29,000,000 of the total, and magazine advertising $24,000,000. Paid advertising enables newspapers and magazines to be sold at lower prices and become available to more people helping to improve living by suggesting more nourishing food, more attractive clothes and homes.

Printing has helped to promote religion among the peoples of the world. Religion is a group undertaking based on recorded traditions and teachings. Without these forms of printing, religion would be unorganized and unavailable to many people.

The Bible is studied by people everywhere, and the lessons it teaches help them in everyday life and make them stronger. Religion tries to help people discover the important things in life and decide upon the way they will live. These discoveries are then recorded so that they can help millions of people everywhere instead of just a few.

Communication has also benefited from printing. Through printed news, people become aware of the world around them. They know what is happening, not only in their own country, but in other countries of the world. Through the use of printing a person in Australia can communicate with a friend 1,000 miles away. Leaders of various countries can transmit important political developments or election results to other nations, often by using printing.

Printed records from past generations enable us to know the history of mankind. These records also make many more inventions possible; the inventor can use facts that have already been proven to help him. Nations can learn from their former mistakes and from the progress of other countries.

Printing has made a great contribution to culture. Through printing, millions of copies of the great classics or the works of modern writers are available to people everywhere. Great philosophers were able to record their ideas, and these works are still available.

Through printing, people have become more aware of the earth's problems. The news media, which include newspapers, magazines, and pamphlets, are mostly responsible for this. There are more than 10,000 newspapers and almost 10,000 magazines being printed in the United States today. Almost 8,000 of the newspapers are weeklies, and dailies make up most of the remainder.

Newspapers give people everywhere facts on the world's happenings so they can vote intelligently for candidates for office and on other issues. Since a democracy depends on the voters being informed, printing plays a large part in government.

Newspapers are first to report to some people the latest world developments. Radio and Television may report the news the quickest, but many people rely on newspapers and magazines for the complete report.

Newspapers notified the world of Charles A. Lindbergh's celebrated transatlantic flight and of Edward H. White's historic walk in space. Newspapers also keep the world informed on rising hemlines and falling necklines, not to mention the newest singing sensations such as Elton John or the Osmond Brothers.

One could say that the magazines are the editorials of printing. In addition to news, stories or novels, editorials, and advertisements, magazines carry feature articles that enlighten the public on a variety of issues, from water pollution to civil rights.

Despite all of printing's good points, some abuses have arisen that should be corrected. Much obscene literature is printed, filling the newsstands with the worst kind of trash. Also, some advertisers take advantage of the consumer by filling their ads with propaganda. Nevertheless, it is obvious that the advantages of printing far outnumber the disadvantages.

Our culture would be very different had we not had the printed word. The great literary masters—Shakespeare, Horace, Keats, Shelley, Dante, etc.—would be unknown to us if our world had lacked the bridge into the past, the printed word.

Because of the printed word, the field of journalism has flourished. This book is designed to familiarize the junior high student with journalistic writing and to show how he can contribute to the world of printing.

Author's note: Some of the examples shown here of stories that appeared in student publications include misspellings and other typographical errors that have been marked for corrections by using professional proofreader's markings.

EXERCISES

1. The history of journalism in the United States is a fascinating topic. Several books have been written on the subject. By using library sources do a 300–500 word written report on one of the following: Joseph Pulitzer, William Randolph Hearst, yellow journalism, penny press, wire services (AP, UPI), Adolph Ochs, Horace Greeley, advertising, censorship, correspondents, newspaper chains.

2. Newspapers are being criticized today for irresponsible reporting. Interview a professional journalist and get his ideas on the role of the press in today's society. Is it possible for the press to become too powerful?

Chapter II

ELEMENTS OF STYLE

Journalistic writing, like any other writing, must follow the rules of English. However, it differs somewhat from that of a school theme, a short story, or other types of writing. Certain rules of style are followed by all newspapers, although each newspaper has its own individual style.

Consistency and *brevity* are two key words to remember in journalistic writing. If months of the year are abbreviated once in a newspaper, for example, they should always be abbreviated.

Each school newspaper should have its own editorial policy as well as style. The following points should be kept in mind when considering the adoption of an editorial policy:

(1) The purpose of a paper is to inform, to entertain, to influence, to recognize, to reflect upon, and to unify the students, faculty, and administration of the school.

(2) The school paper should reserve the right to criticize anything constructively, as long as it is to the interest of all.

(3) The school paper should not print, in any manner or form, news that could downgrade or tarnish the reputation of an individual or a group.

(4) The school paper should give full recognition and credit to students, faculty, and administration with regard to scholastic achievement.

(5) The school newspaper should give recognition and credit to students, faculty, and administration with regard to extra-curricular activities.

(6) The school paper should always practice journalistic honesty.

(7) The school paper should present, fairly, openly, and clearly, views on controversial issues.

(8) The school paper should use a by-line when recognition

is earned, with special recognition of those reporters outside the journalism class.

(9) The school paper should maintain the policy that the paper is published for the good of the community, which includes teachers, administrators, students, parents, and other local residents.

By following the above editorial policy guidelines and adopting and using good style, any school can have a good paper. The school should have its own stylebook, and every student should familiarize himself with its rules in order to be sure of writing his stories correctly.

All copy should be written in ink or typewritten double-spaced on 8½" × 11" paper.

In the upper left corner of each page of the story the student should place his name, the name of the story (guideline), and his class. The guideline should be just long enough to identify the story. For example, if you were writing a story on the Science Club's field trip to Babler Park, your guideline might be "Science Trip."

In the upper right corner of the first page of the copy, the number of words in the story should be entered. This is necessary in order to determine the number of inches the story will cover in print. Approximately 40 words will make one inch.

Begin the story itself halfway down the first page. This is necessary in order to leave room for rewriting the lead if necessary, and for giving directions to the typists.

At the end of each page write the word "more" and at the end of the story write "30" or the symbol #. These symbols tell the typists and the printers that this is the end of the story.

All of the above-mentioned symbols should be circled so they stand out and are easy to locate. All directions to the printer should also be circled.

Style rules make it easier for the reader to follow a story, and they also make it easier for the reporter to write a story.

The following rules are offered as suggestions for a school newspaper stylebook.

CAPITALIZATION

1. Capitalize titles preceding names. Do not capitalize titles standing alone or following names, except President, when President of the United States or any other nation is meant.

2. Do not capitalize occupational titles.

3. Capitalize the names of all races and nationalities. EXAMPLES: Mexicans, French.

4. Capitalize the important words in titles of books, poems, music, articles, plays, lecture topics, and chapter titles, including the initial articles *A, An,* or *The.* EXAMPLE: The title of the book was *The Seat of Power.*

5. Capitalize the names of units of government. EXAMPLES: General Assembly, Senate, City Council, Board of Aldermen.

6. Do not capitalize names of administrative offices.

7. Do not capitalize school board or board of education.

8. Do not capitalize names of school subjects, except languages. EXAMPLES: German, general science.

9. Do not capitalize names of school classes. EXAMPLES: seventh grade, eighth grade, freshman.

10. Capitalize names of athletic teams. EXAMPLES: Pioneers, Tigers.

11. Do not capitalize the word *varsity* unless it is part of a headline or the first word in a sentence.

12. Do not capitalize the names of buildings unless the complete official title is used.

13. Do not capitalize the word *room.* EXAMPLE: room 24.

14. Capitalize all parts of the names of clubs, associations, roads, streets, schools, school departments, companies, universities, colleges, rivers, and similar items. EXAMPLES: Social Studies Department, Jefferson Street, Mississippi River, Pep Club, North

Central Accrediting Association. Do not capitalize second and succeeding references. EXAMPLE: Science Club; the club elected officers.

15. Capitalize college degrees when abbreviated but not when spelled out. EXAMPLES: B.S., M.S., bachelor of science.

16. Capitalize the months and days of the week.

17. Do not capitalize seasons of the year.

18. Capitalize special occasions and holidays. EXAMPLES: Sweatshirt Day, Christmas.

19. Capitalize the abbreviations for post meridiem and ante meridiem. EXAMPLE: The time is 11 P.M.

20. Capitalize sections of the country, but not compass directions. EXAMPLE: He toured the South. The track faces north.

ABBREVIATIONS

1. Abbreviate without spaces or periods the names of groups, government agencies, military or civil organizations, radio stations, time zones, etc. EXAMPLES: KXOK, PTA, GAA, YMCA.

2. Abbreviate types of business firms. EXAMPLES: Corp., Inc., Co.

3. In addresses, abbreviate: St., Blvd., Ave., Ter., Pl., Sq.

4. Abbreviate names of states when immediately following names of cities and towns. EXAMPLES: St. Louis, Mo.; New York, N.Y.

5. Do not abbreviate names of states when they stand alone.

6. Do not abbreviate names of foreign countries. Note exceptions in No. 7.

7. Abbreviate United Nations, United States (as an adjective) and Union of Soviet Socialist Republics, with periods but without space. EXAMPLES: U.N., U.S., U.S.S.R.

8. Do not abbreviate United States when used as a noun.

9. Abbreviate religious, fraternal, scholastic, or honorary degrees used after the name of an individual; use capitals and periods.

10. Abbreviate the following titles when they precede names: Mister, Mistress, Doctor, Reverend. EXAMPLES: Mr. Walter Stokes, Mrs. Walter Stokes, Dr. Walter Stokes. Always supply the word *the* before Reverend.

11. Abbreviate months when used with a specific date but not when standing alone. EXAMPLES: Monday, Feb. 11. The event occurred in February.

12. Do not abbreviate days of the week.

13. Do not abbreviate Christmas as Xmas.

14. Abbreviate *number* before figures. EXAMPLE: No. 10 just left the game.

15. Abbreviate *junior* or *senior* following a name but do not use a comma. EXAMPLE: John Jones Jr.

16. Do not begin a sentence with an abbreviation except in the case of Mr., Mrs., or Dr. followed by a name.

17. Abbreviate long names of organizations when there can be no confusion, but spell out the name the first time it appears in the story.

NAMES

1. The first time a woman member of the faculty is mentioned in a story, use the complete name preceded by Miss, Mrs., or her title.

2. The second and succeeding times a woman teacher's name is mentioned, use the appropriate title followed by the last name.

3. The first time a male member of the faculty is mentioned, use the complete name preceded by Mr. or the appropriate title.

4. The second and succeeding times, use the appropriate title followed by the last name only. EXCEPTION: Never say Principal Thomas; *second* reference: Mr. Thomas.

5. The rules for names of faculty members apply to names of school administrative officials or any other adults whether concerned with the school or not.

6. The first time a student's name is given, use the full name as he is accustomed to giving it; do not use Mr., Miss, or Mrs.

7. The second and succeeding times a student's name is mentioned, use the first name only. However, in sports stories, use the last name only.

8. Titles, if short, precede the name and are capitalized.

9. Titles or phrases of identification of more than two words follow the name and are not capitalized.

10. Identify a person the first time he is mentioned in the story.

11. Avoid pointless use of two titles. Don't write Mr. B. L. Thomas, principal, but do write Principal B. L. Thomas.

12. When giving a formalized list of names, as in the case of election results, titles or phrases of identification must always follow the name and be in lower-case letters, regardless of the length.

13. In giving complete names, never give the first initial only. The full first name and middle initial are preferred, but initials may be used for first and second names.

14. Use both Mr. and Mrs. when referring to a man and his wife. EXAMPLE: Mr. and Mrs. Jack Jones.

15. Nicknames should be enclosed in quotation marks.

16. Use the title professor only for college or university teachers who hold the title.

NUMBERS

1. With the exceptions noted below, spell out numbers under 10. Use figures for those over 10, except for some round numbers, which may be spelled out. EXAMPLE: He spent two million dollars.

2. Use figures for numbers under 10 when in a series with numbers over 10.

3. Spell out ninth, eighth, seventh, etc., when referring to grades.

4. Use figures for ages, dimensions, room numbers, scores, prices, degrees, percents, time ratings, and hours of the day.

5. Do not use the sign for percent; spell it out.

6. In dates do not add "th," "rd," "nd," and "st" to the figures.

7. Do not use figures to begin a sentence. Figures may be used to begin a headline but should be avoided if possible.

8. Do not hyphenate scores in sports stories, except in the headline. EXAMPLE: North edged South, 50 to 49.

9. Use figures and the word cent or cents for money values under one dollar. Use figures and the dollar sign for values over one dollar.

10. Do not use the colon for even hours. EXAMPLE: The game began at 6 P.M.

11. Do not use the decimal point for even amounts of money. EXAMPLE: He earned $10 for the week.

12. Spell out the number of a century.

13. Spell out fractions.

14. Use the words noon or midnight, not 12 noon or 12 midnight or 12 P.M. or 12 A.M.

15. When writing time, date, and place in a story, always give them in that order.

16. Spell out the words inches, feet, pounds, degrees, and other units of measurement.

PUNCTUATION

COMMA

1. Use the comma to separate all words in a series.

2. Use the comma to set off sports scores.

3. Use the comma to set off phrases of identification or appositives.

4. Use the comma to indicate the omission of a verb.

5. Use the comma to separate two adjectives when they modify the same noun with equal force.

6. Omit the comma before Roman numerals, Jr., Sr., and street addresses.

7. Omit the comma in such expressions as "16 years 6 months old" and "10 feet 8 inches high."

SEMICOLON

1. Use the semicolon to separate phrases containing commas, statements of contrasts, and statements too closely related.

2. Use the semicolon to separate clauses in which the conjunction is omitted.

3. Do not use a semicolon where a period will serve the same purpose.

COLON

1. Use the colon to introduce listings, statements, and texts.

2. Use the colon after the introduction of a quotation of one or more paragraphs.

3. Use the colon in stating time in a track event.

4. Begin a new paragraph after the colon, if the list that follows is long.

5. Use the colon in clock time.

6. Use the colon after the word "Resolved," when stating the topic of a debate.

HYPHEN

1. Use the hyphen with compound adjectives.

2. Use the hyphen in headlines to indicate sports scores.

QUOTATION MARKS

1. Do not use quotation marks for titles of books, plays, magazines, or newspapers. Underline them to indicate that they are to be set in italics.

2. Use quotation marks for titles of magazine or newspaper articles, pamphlets, and chapters.

3. In a quotation consisting of more than one paragraph, use quotation marks at the beginning of each paragraph but only at the end of the last paragraph.

4. In a quotation within a quotation, use single quote marks for the inside quotation.

5. Semicolons, question marks, and exclamation points follow the quotation marks unless they are part of the quoted material, in which case they are placed inside the quotation marks.

6. Use quotation marks to indicate words or expressions used out of their usual context or with a special meaning.

APOSTROPHE

1. Use an apostrophe and an *s* to indicate possession in singular and plural nouns that do not end in *s*. EXAMPLES: boy's shorts; Margie's book.

2. Use the apostrophe alone to indicate possession in singular or plural nouns that end in *s*. EXAMPLE: boys' shorts; Jim Valais' room.

3. Use the apostrophe to indicate omitted letters and numbers. EXAMPLE: In '68 rainfall totaled 34 inches.

4. Use the apostrophe and an *s* to form plurals of figures.

5. The possessive form of personal pronouns such as *its* and *ours* do not take the apostrophe.

PARENTHESES

1. Where location identification is needed but is not part of the official name, parentheses are used. EXAMPLE: St. Louis (Missouri) Association of Bankers.

2. Divisions of text material should be enclosed in parentheses. EX-AMPLE: Three rules must be followed: (1) don't run in the halls; (2) don't push or shove; and (3) keep your hair short.

The above style rules are not meant to be all-inclusive. They may be expanded or altered as desired. The main purpose of establishing a style is to make possible consistency and accuracy in the school paper.

The quality of the student journalist's work reflects not only on himself but also on the entire staff, the rest of the student body, the school, and the community.

Knowing the style rules will enable the members of the staff to produce a paper of which they and the school can be proud.

EXERCISES

Based on the above style rules do the following exercises.

1. Rewrite the following sentences to conform to the rules of style. In some sentences there is more than one style error. Assume the sentences are leads.

(a) Mr. John Lewis told a group of students yesterday that they have a tremendous responsibility to perform in society.

(b) The science club put on an excellent demonstration about bugs yesterday in the cafetorium.

(c) I attended the Pep Club meeting and thought it was the best one held all year, said Mary Worth.

(d) Jack Sharp, history teacher, has been awarded a fellowship to Washington University for next summer.

(e) There were 15 members of the Girl's Glee Club, five members of the Pep club, 10 members of the Science club, and fifteen members of the Projector's Club attending the meeting held to discuss the possibility of combining their efforts to start a campaign for the purchase of additional football bleachers.

(f) Mr. Joe Bailey, principal, recently returned from a one-week convention held in Columbia, Mo.

(g) At 10:00 a.m. last Fri. an explosion occurred in Jim Valais' science room, Room 24.

(h) The course biology is being offered for the first time this year.

(i) The journalism department will hold a writing contest next Fri. at 3:00 P.M. in Room 23.

(j) Tacky Day will be held on November 24th.

(k) The Spring All-School Dance will have as its theme Harvest Moon.

(l) Joe Brown is a large aggressive tackle who should be a big help to this years' team.

(m) Jim Hill, president of the student council, will speak to the student body concerning school spirit in next weeks assembly.

(n) Twenty one students from North entered projects in this year's science fair.

(o) Paul Benson caught the ball on the 30 yard line. Paul Benson then went on to score the only touchdown of the game, making the only score 7–0.

(p) Miss Joan Fenton, ninth grader, has been announced as the winner in Kirkwood's Green Tree Contest.

2. Rewrite the following stories to conform to style rules.

(a) North's science club held its first meeting in Mr. Smith's room on Sept. 21st at 4:00 P.M.
An element collection is the main project of the club this year, and Mr. John Filer and Jerry Ealer have been appointed Chairmen to head the project.
It is hoped that at least fifty-five elements can be collected by the end of the year.

(b) North was beaten decisively 14–0 in their first football game of the season at Brentwood. Jerry Lepor scored both touchdowns for Brentwood. Jerry scored on a 10 yard run and on a 2 yard plunge.

Norths only serious drive was made in the 4th quarter but was stalled on the 5 yard line when the game ended.

Bill Strattman, Norths quarterback was the leading ground gainer of the game as he rushed for fifty-five yards. Bill also connected on 8 passes for another 40 yards.

(c) Student Council officers were elected yesterday by the student body. The president is Bill Snow, the vice-president is Jody McMillan. Bill Dupes is the secretary and the treasurer is John Hall. All four of the officers are 9th graders, and all 4 served on the student council in the 7th and 8th grades.

Snow announced that he had many plans for the Student Council this year and that he hoped, the students would support the council by offering suggestions on how they might improve themselves.

Snow received 432 votes, and his opponent Mr. Jack Red received 327 votes.

(d) Jerry Jacobs won first place in a writing contest held at Missouri university on December 20th.

Jacobs was competing with other Freshmen in a news-writing contest. He scored ninety-five out of one hundred possible points. The judging was done by 5 newspaper sponsors throughout the state. The news story dealt with Mr. Joe Carson, Senator from Mo., and he made a visit to the school.

Jacobs received a book entitled Have No Fear along with a certificate.

3. The following lead sentences have capitalization errors only. Correct the errors according to style rules.

(a) Last saturday, principal E. L. Smith attended a Convention of School Principals at Columbia, Missouri.

(b) Jill Gibault read the book *From here to eternity.*

(c) Pep club, science club, Debate club, and English Club are planning to sponsor a school carnival in March.

(d) Mr. Ted Seco, Citizenship teacher, received his Bachelor of Science Degree from Meramec College.

(e) The Freshman class will hold a dance next Friday in the Cafetorium.

(f) The Varsity Football Team defeated Steger junior high last Monday.

4. The following sentences contain errors in abbreviations only. Correct the sentences according to style rules.

(a) The P.T.A. will meet on Thursday night to see a demonstration by the G.A.A.

(b) The location of the next track meet is Beloit Junior High, which is at 1133 North Street.

(c) Saint Louis, Mo., was the topic of discussion in the seventh-grade core classes last week, the 21st of Apr.

(d) Next Wed., Jim Chapman will wrestle Bob Burns, and on Thurs. the winner will meet Jack Jay.

(e) Bill Tatum Junior and Bob Well Senior placed 1st and second in the 22-yard dash.

5. The following exercises have errors in name usage only. Correct the sentences according to style rules.

(a) Debbie Smith, Spanish teacher, and Tom Schmidt, art teacher, will sing a duet in the faculty talent show to be given on Friday. Smith and Schmidt both have minors in music.

(b) Mrs. Shull, ninth-grade English teacher, has agreed to sponsor a Debate Club. Shull plans to hold an initial meeting on Tuesday.

(c) W. L. Clay, principal, presented a proposal to Steve Soell, ninth-grade class president, on how to get more student participation in class activities. Soell plans to present the proposal to Bill Brown, ninth-grade history teacher and sponsor of the ninth-grade class.

(d) Dave Schafer scored two touchdowns and Gary Olson one in last Friday's game. Dave scored on a 10-yard run and a 20-yard pass play, and Olson drove over from the one. Gary also converted all three extra points.

(e) W. Lewton and F. Browne were chosen as Speakers of the House in H. T. Matthews' citizenship classes. Mr. H. T. Matthews is holding mock Congresses in his classes.

6. The following sentences contain errors in use of numbers. Correct the sentences according to style rules.

(a) The 9th, 8th, and 7th grades have 2 committees each working on the dance scheduled for February 15th.

(b) Bob Jones, fourteen years old, and Bill Bates, 13 years old, are winners of the local pass, punt, and kick contest in which twenty-five boys participated on March 13th.

(c) At 3:00 P.M. tomorrow and at 4 P.M. on Friday pictures will be taken for the yearbook.

(d) Approximately ⅓ of North's students will attend the next basketball game, which will begin at 4:00 P.M. on December 2nd.

7. The following sentences contain errors in punctuation only. Make corrections according to style rules.

(a) The tallest player on Easts' squad is 6 feet 1 inch tall.

(b) The following students have been selected for the cast of the next ninth-grade play; Bob Wells, Bob Maloy, Frank Thomas June Litch and Susan Free.

(c) Mr. Joe Bailey state representative spoke to Mr. Bill Hailey's citizenship class on Thursday. The topic of his speech was how to Improve State Legislatures."

(d) "The next assembly will be Thursday said Principal Elmer Safus.

(e) Three rules govern the contest; 1. All material must be original. 2. No entry may be more than 500 words. 3. All entries must be typewritten.

8. Discuss the editorial policy given on pages 14 and 15. Then write an editorial policy for your own newspaper adding to those given in the book.

9. In teams of two or three, or individually, devise an editorial policy for your school publications.

Chapter III

WRITING A NEWS STORY

Now that you have learned the style rules you should be able to write a good news story.

Before you can begin to write a news story, however, you must know what news is. NEWS can be defined as a hitherto unpublished report of any activity designed to inform the readers. As such, the event should be of some importance.

Several factors must be taken into consideration before writing a news story. The news qualities of ACCURACY, CONCISE-NESS, OBJECTIVENESS, BALANCE, and TIMELINESS are important.

There is no place for inaccurate statements in a school newspaper. Inaccurate statements are misleading to the readers and the newspaper has the function of serving the readers. Accuracy means having all facts correct. This includes the spelling of every name correctly, having all dates exact, and correct quotes.

Student reporters should get in the habit of always checking with the staff member involved with a story for accurate facts. DO NOT rely on friends for accurate information.

Sometimes it may be necessary to use reference sources to obtain accurate information. Use dictionaries and encyclopedias whenever you are in doubt of facts in a story.

The quality of brevity or conciseness was discussed in Chapter II. All news stories should be concise but accurate.

To obtain balance in a news story the reporter must make sure that all his facts are complete. The reader should never be left with questions in his mind after reading a story. At the same time the reporter must be objective in his writing. Objective reporting means that personal bias is left out. To a certain extent this is impossible as no two reporters will see a story in the same

Grand Jury finds SUSD in trouble

Fraud, embezzlement, and corruption in Stockton Unified School Dsitrict were disclosed last month in the 1981-82 County Grand Jury report after a year-long investigation of the financial condition of the district.

The Grand Jury also called for the resignation of six of the school board and the school superintendent, George Xenos.

The board members, Barbara Walker, Booker Guyton, Margaret Shelton, Ann Stallworth, Fred Godinez, Betty Payne, and Xenos have all refused to resign, claiming that the report gives an unclear picture of the district's problems.

The trustees were already aware of criminal wrongdoing by employees as they had encouraged investigation of the district's business operations.

Some district personnel have already been dismissed as a result. The Dictrict Attorney's office has been checking into these problems with indictments to follow their investigation.

Support of the SUSD trustees and superintendent has come from the Lincoln board this month in the form of a published letter in the *Stockton Record*. The letter said that facts stated by the Grand Jury do not support their conclusions for the resignation of the SUSD trustees and superintendent.

The Grand Jury recommendations have created much concern and instability for school personnel, parents, and students in the district. People have responded with differing views in letters to the local newspaper, some asking for recall of the Board and some support both Xenos and the trustees.

The school board and superintendent are asking district personnel to "ride out" the first wave of concern about SUSD's problems.

After criminal indictments have been filed by the District Attorney, then all facts will surface and a clearer picture of the district's problems will appear.

Publications push fund-raising projects

Video games and buttons are the money-making projects of the journalism and yearbook classes.

Four video games, football, bowling, Space Wars, and Depthcharge, are used by students during both lunch periods only. They offer students a couple of challenging minutes against a computer for a quarter.

Personalized buttons, which is a year-long project, can be ordered in Room 104 during both lunch periods for 75 cents. The button must be paid for in advance and will be ready for pickup the next day.

Jiang wins seventh grade representative office

By Candice Perry

Cecilia Jiang came out the winner for the office of seventh grade representative after election results were announced on October 19.

One other student, Vicky Flaig, ran for this office. Jiang is a member of the student leadership class and will attend all Student Council meetings where she will bring seventh grade problems and interests to the attention of the Council members.

"Right now, I don't do anything special, but my plans are for equal rights at this school," said Jiang.

Variety in types of news stories is important. The Webster Warrior, *Daniel Webster Middle School, Stockton, California, has obtained this variety by covering a controversial situation, money-making activities, and an election on the same page.*

way but there is no place in journalism for biased reporting done on purpose.

You should be especially concerned with news of interest to a junior-high student. However, this does not mean that only school events should be reported. Many things occurring outside the school will also be of interest to students. It is important that *all* such news be reported.

Timeliness is sometimes hard to achieve when the paper is issued monthly. An event that occurs the day after publication cannot be reported until the next month's issue. However, the paper can carry a news item that the event is to occur and then a follow-up story in the next issue describing what took place. When an advance story is used, a follow-up story is necessary, even if the news is a month old.

The first essential in writing a news story is an appropriate lead. Your lead must gain the reader's attention and interest or he will not read the rest of the story.

It is essential that the lead contain the important facts of the story. Few people have time to read all the stories in a newspaper; however, if the lead contains the essential information, the reader can scan the leads and get a quick picture of the news. If the lead is written interestingly, the reader is likely to finish the entire story. If the lead is dull and provides no excitement, he is likely to pass on to the next story. Therefore, it is important that the lead be written interestingly and that it contain the most important facts.

The lead of a news story is actually a summary of that story. The summary should include at least one of the five W's and the one H of news writing—Who, What, Where, When, Why, and How. It may be necessary at times to add a seventh—Who Says So. Not all leads necessarily contain all six W's and the one H. It is up to you, the reporter, to decide which are the most important.

A lead with all the W's and one H is referred to as the "AP lead" as the Associated Press used it for many years. It is also known as the "clothesline" lead because it was long and heavy.

When radio came into existence it made it necessary for newspapers to reduce the length of their lead to remain in competition.

The first three or four words of a lead denote the most important part of the story. If you start with a person, you are using a Who lead.

You may begin your lead with any of the six W's or the H. The one you choose will depend upon the story you are writing. A When or Where lead is seldom used. Most people do not care

Yearbook distribution, signing party on June 1

By Glenda Taylor

Yearbooks will be distributed on Wed., June 1, during period seven to students and teachers who have ordered a copy of the 1983 *Paragon*. A Signing Party will be held in the cafeteria from 2 to 4:30 p.m. for those who wish to get all their friends' autographs.

No admission will be charged, but the student store will be open to sell drinks, food, and pens. An activity bus will leave the campus at around 3 p.m.

"Yearbooks cannot be signed during classtime, so the best way to get autographs is to come to the Signing Party," said Hilda Walker, yearbook adviser.

Students who purchased yearbooks with their name stamped in gold on the cover will get a free plastic cover and one eight-page autograph folder. Extra autograph pages will be sold at the Signing Party for 50 cents. Plastic covers will cost $1.00

All people who ordered yearbooks should start looking for the receipt they were given when they bought the book. Anyone who has lost his/her receipt, or it has been stolen, should put their name on a list in Room 14 or 104, or contact Walker during both lunch periods, before, or after school.

Replacement receipts will be given out on Tuesday, May 31. They must be brought to school the next day as this receipt is the student's hall pass to get out of class to pick up the yearbook. If the receipt is forgotten, students can still get their book, but must wait until the end of seventh period.

About 100 extra yearbooks have been ordered and are now on sale for $10 to the first people to bring the money to Room 104. This sale is by cash or check only to the first 100 students to request that a book be saved for them.

A good "What" lead is illustrated by the above news story from Webster Warrior, *Daniel Webster Middle School, Stockton, California. The rest of the story is written in inverted pyramid style, enabling the last paragraphs to be cut if necessary.*

First Time In 30 Years :

Highlights Breaks Record Earning "Medalist" Award

by Marybeth Beach

The "Medalist Award," an exclusive award offered by the Columbia Scholastic Press Association for outstanding achievement by a school newspaper, has been presented to **Highlights** for the first time in Edison's history.

Competing with over **2,000** newspapers, the publication was one of four newspapers in its category which received the award, a special consideration and high honor which is given to a few selected newspapers.

Highlights was judged in a category for offset newspapers in junior high schools with enrollment of 701 to 1200 pupils.

"Excellent coverage" and an "adviser in the know" were principal reasons for the success of the publication. The paper also concentrated on improving layout, headlines and photography.

Highlights received 940 out of 1000 points in the judging.

The last two issues of the 1965-66 **Highlights**, edited by Peggy Mitchell, and the first three issues of the 1966-67 **Highlights**, edited by Karla Anderson, were reviewed.

The following students are presently working on the editorial staff: Anita Hankinson, Managing Editor; Marybeth Beach, News Editor; Peggy Smith, Feature Editor; and Marc Changnon and Steve La Rocque, Sports Editors.

Mrs. Melinda Foys was the paper's new faculty adviser last year, and has continued in that position this year.

A "What" lead is demonstrated in the above news story from Highlights, Edison Junior High School, Champaign, Illinois. The headline also demonstrates the effective use of a kicker.

Drastic Changes For R-2 If Levy Fails Once More

Because of a failure to meet a 2/3 majority, the tax levy, which obtained a 60% majority vote, failed once again to pass on Tuesday, April 6th. The vote was for a 29c tax increase for the schools. The failure means that there will be some changes if the increase again fails when it is put up once more in a special election on the fourth of May. This time the increase will be 34c and will go for hiring new and keeping old teachers and keeping classes a reasonable size as the schools make way for many more students next year.

There will be no book fees next year if it passes, and also at least 6 other things will be changed to make up the shortage:

1. The bus-riding boundary will be moved from a mile to a mile and a half.

2. The book fee will be raised to $15.00 for each junior and senior student

3. A material fee of $4.00 for each elementary pupil will be charged.

4. There again will be no kindergarten.

5. All junior high athletics will be cancelled.

6. All non-instructional activities and use of the school buildings by outside organizations will be discontinued.

A substantive-clause lead is illustrated by the above news story from The Torch, *Ferguson Junior High School, Ferguson, Missouri. It also indicates how a school paper can serve as a public relations instrument.*

when or where an event took place but are more interested in what happened or who was involved. Quite often, time and place belong in the lead paragraph but not in the first three or four words. When writing time and place, remember that time should always go before place.

"Lonesome Train"
Honors Abe Lincoln

". . He did what everybody likes to do sometimes when they're tired. He went to a show....And along about the middle of the evening, something happened that wasn't on the program. . . ."

These lines were spoken by the narrator to set the mood for "The Lonesome Train," a cantata, which was presented by the Irving Fine Arts Department on Friday, February 12. Two performances were presented: one in an assembly that morning, the second at 8:00 in the evening.

"The Lonesome Train" is the story of the encounters of President Lincoln's funeral train, traveling from Washington, D.C., to Springfield, Illinois. As the train moved from one town to another, the audience saw the various reactions of the people in these towns to Abraham Lincoln's death.

In one segment of "The Lonesome Train", a service in a small church was shown. Perhaps this was one way the people showed their feelings towards President Lincoln. The preacher was played by Mike Turner, and the quartet was Nancy Kroger, Lin Gowin, Doug Balok and Rich Ganz. The square dance section was a switch to a more light-hearted mood. The square dance caller was Steve Martens, and the square dancers were from Mixed Chorus.

Abraham Lincoln was played by Greg Brown. The narrator for the morning performance was Liz Knoll; Libby Swanson narrated in the evening. The ballad singers were Lee Lukehart and Greg Rullifson, who emphasized what the narrator had spoken. There were also small solos from members of the chorus.

The production was directed by Mr. Max Bottger. Mrs. Sally Jerome was in charge of the vocal music, and Mrs. Dean Frost supplied various speaking parts with members of her second period drama class. The art work was provided by some of the students in Miss Margaret Furlong's art class. The square dance was choreographed by Miss Gayla Anderson, student teacher for Mrs. Frost.

Quotes often make good variety leads for news stories. Make sure the quote is appropriate to the story though. The above is from the Irving News, *Irving Jr. High, Lincoln, Nebraska.*

Leads should be colorful and complete but avoid wordiness and should be limited to one main idea. Get to the point as soon as possible, but be careful not to leave out any essential information. Paragraphs should not exceed 40 words in length. However, leads may be more than one paragraph in length, although usually this is not necessary. Most leads today are one sentence in length.

The only test for the adequacy of the lead is whether it gives the reader the bare outlines of the story.

Most leads are written in the order of English sentences, which is subject, verb, and object or predicate noun or adjective. It is not necessary, however, that all news leads be written this way. Variety is important. From your study of English you know that sentences can be written in different orders.

There are many ways to achieve variety in leads. Leads may

when or where an event took place but are more interested in what happened or who was involved. Quite often, time and place belong in the lead paragraph but not in the first three or four words. When writing time and place, remember that time should always go before place.

"Lonesome Train"
Honors Abe Lincoln

"..He did what everybody likes to do sometimes when they're tired. He went to a show....And along about the middle of the evening, something happened that wasn't on the program...."

These lines were spoken by the narrator to set the mood for "The Lonesome Train," a cantata, which was presented by the Irving Fine Arts Department on Friday, February 12. Two performances were presented: one in an assembly that morning, the second at 8:00 in the evening.

"The Lonesome Train" is the story of the encounters of President Lincoln's funeral train, traveling from Washington, D.C., to Springfield, Illinois. As the

train moved from one town to another, the audience saw the various reactions of the people in these towns to Abraham Lincoln's death.

In one segment of "The Lonesome Train", a service in a small church was shown. Perhaps this was one way the people showed their feelings towards President Lincoln. The preacher was played by Mike Turner, and the quartet was Nancy Kroger, Lin Gowin, Doug Balok and Rich Ganz. The square dance section was a switch to a more light-hearted mood. The square dance caller was Steve Martens, and the square dancers were from Mixed Chorus.

Abraham Lincoln was played by Greg Brown. The narrator for

the morning performance was Liz Knoll; Libby Swanson narrated in the evening. The ballad singers were Lee Lukehart and Greg Rullifson, who emphasized what the narrator had spoken. There were also small solos from members of the chorus.

The production was directed by Mr. Max Bottger. Mrs. Sally Jerome was in charge of the vocal music, and Mrs. Dean Frost supplied various speaking parts with members of her second period drama class. The art work was provided by some of the students in Miss Margaret Furlong's art class. The square dance was choreographed by Miss Gayla Anderson, student teacher for Mrs. Frost.

Quotes often make good variety leads for news stories. Make sure the quote is appropriate to the story though. The above is from the Irving News, *Irving Jr. High, Lincoln, Nebraska.*

Leads should be colorful and complete but avoid wordiness and should be limited to one main idea. Get to the point as soon as possible, but be careful not to leave out any essential information. Paragraphs should not exceed 40 words in length. However, leads may be more than one paragraph in length, although usually this is not necessary. Most leads today are one sentence in length.

The only test for the adequacy of the lead is whether it gives the reader the bare outlines of the story.

Most leads are written in the order of English sentences, which is subject, verb, and object or predicate noun or adjective. It is not necessary, however, that all news leads be written this way. Variety is important. From your study of English you know that sentences can be written in different orders.

There are many ways to achieve variety in leads. Leads may

When radio came into existence it made it necessary for newspapers to reduce the length of their lead to remain in competition.

The first three or four words of a lead denote the most important part of the story. If you start with a person, you are using a Who lead.

You may begin your lead with any of the six W's or the H. The one you choose will depend upon the story you are writing. A When or Where lead is seldom used. Most people do not care

Yearbook distribution, signing party on June 1

By Glenda Taylor

Yearbooks will be distributed on Wed., June 1, during period seven to students and teachers who have ordered a copy of the 1983 *Paragon*. A Signing Party will be held in the cafeteria from 2 to 4:30 p.m. for those who wish to get all tl.eir friends' autographs.

No admission will be charged, but the student store will be open to sell drinks, food, and pens. An activity bus will leave the campus at around 3 p.m.

"Yearbooks cannot be signed during classtime, so the best way to get autographs is to come to the Signing Party," said Hilda Walker, yearbook adviser.

Students who purchased yearbooks with their name stamped in gold on the cover will get a free plastic cover and one eight-page autograph folder. Extra autograph pages will be sold at the Signing Party for 50 cents. Plastic covers will cost $1.00

All people who ordered yearbooks should start looking for the receipt they were given when they bought the book. Anyone who has lost his/her receipt, or it has been stolen, should put their name on a list in Room 14 or 104, or contact Walker during both lunch periods, before, or after school.

Replacement receipts will be given out on Tuesday, May 31. They must be brought to school the next day as this receipt is the student's hall pass to get out of class to pick up the yearbook. If the receipt is forgotten, students can still get their book, but must wait until the end of seventh period.

About 100 extra yearbooks have been ordered and are now on sale for $10 to the first people to bring the money to Room 104. This sale is by cash or check only to the first 100 students to request that a book be saved for them.

A good "What" lead is illustrated by the above news story from Webster Warrior, *Daniel Webster Middle School, Stockton, California. The rest of the story is written in inverted pyramid style, enabling the last paragraphs to be cut if necessary.*

First Time In 30 Years :

Highlights Breaks Record Earning "Medalist" Award

by Marybeth Beach

The "Medalist Award," an exclusive award offered by the Columbia Scholastic Press Association for outstanding achievement by a school newspaper, has been presented to **Highlights** for the first time in Edison's history.

Competing with over 2,000 newspapers, the publication was one of four newspapers in its category which received the award, a special consideration and high honor which is given to a few selected newspapers.

Highlights was judged in a category for offset newspapers in junior high schools with enrollment of 701 to 1200 pupils. "Excellent coverage" and an "adviser in the know" were principal reasons for the success of the publication. The paper also concentrated on improving layout, headlines and photography.

Highlights received 940 out of 1000 points in the judging.

The last two issues of the 1965-66 **Highlights**, edited by Peggy Mitchell, and the first three issues of the 1966-67 **Highlights**, edited by Karla Anderson, were reviewed.

The following students are presently working on the editorial staff: Anita Hankinson, Managing Editor; Marybeth Beach, News Editor; Peggy Smith, Feature Editor; and Marc Changnon and Steve La Rocque, Sports Editors.

Mrs. Melinda Foys was the paper's new faculty adviser last year, and has continued in that position this year.

A "What" lead is demonstrated in the above news story from Highlights, Edison Junior High School, Champaign, Illinois. The headline also demonstrates the effective use of a kicker.

Drastic Changes For R-2 If Levy Fails Once More

Because of a failure to meet a 2/3 majority, the tax levy, which obtained a 60% majority vote, failed once again to pass on Tuesday, April 6th. The vote was for a 29c tax increase for the schools. The failure means that there will be some changes if the increase again fails when it is put up once more in a special election on the fourth of May. This time the increase will be 34c and will go for hiring new and keeping old teachers and keeping classes a reasonable size as the schools make way for many more students next year.

There will be no book fees next year if it passes, and also at least 6 other things will be changed to make up the shortage:

1. The bus-riding boundary will be moved from a mile to a mile and a half.

2. The book fee will be raised to $15.00 for each junior and senior student

3. A material fee of $4.00 for each elementary pupil will be charged.

4. There again will be no kindergarten.

5. All junior high athletics will be cancelled.

6. All non-instructional activities and use of the school buildings by outside organizations will be discontinued.

A substantive-clause lead is illustrated by the above news story from The Torch, Ferguson Junior High School, Ferguson, Missouri. It also indicates how a school paper can serve as a public relations instrument.

begin with gerunds, adverbs, infinitives, participles, or prepositions. The reason why something occurred might also be the basis for the lead. Normally, however, a Who, What, Where, or How lead is the best.

Be sure not to overuse one type of lead. It would be a poor paper that began every story with a Who lead. Too many leads of the same type become monotonous to the reader. No matter which type of lead you choose, keep in mind that clarity, brevity, and accuracy are important.

Flapper Friday --- Day From the Past

On December 15 Hanley students and teachers honored Flapper Friday by wearing clothes which were popular during the Roaring 20's.

Earlier this year the steering committee decided that the theme of this year's carnival was to be based on the 20's.

A "When" lead is illustrated by the above news story from The Acorn, *Hanley Junior High School, University City, Missouri.*

The word "lead" means just what it says. The lead should lead the reader into the rest of the story. Don't lose your reader on that first paragraph! Make it interesting!

Avoid, when possible, beginning a lead with the articles *a, an,* and *the.* A common fault of junior-high papers is starting most stories with an article. This also can become monotonous. Get that most important fact as your first word if at all possible.

The source of the story should be cited in the lead if it is generally unknown to the students. If the story is about an event that most students have witnessed, it is not necessary to cite the source.

How do you write a summary lead? First find the six W's and the H. Next decide which is most important, which will interest your readers the most. Then arrange the remaining five W's and H, or six W's, in order of decreasing importance.

Briefs

Raising funds

In order to raise money for handicapped children, the March of Dimes is sponsoring its annual Walkathon again this year. The 20km walk will take place on April 24. Chaffin has challenged Ramsey, Kimmons, Darby, Northside, and Southside to see who will raise the most money.

Society meets

Honor Society members will be attending a convention in Springdale, Arkansas in May. The convention will feature Honor Society presidents from this area speaking on past events. A banquet will close the convention.

Riverfest coming

The third annual Riverfest is being sponsored by the Junior League of Fort Smith. The Riverfest, which will be held on May 14, 15 and 16 will include games, foods and productions from European and Asian cultures.

Spring concert

All three bands will be featured in the spring concert of the Chaffin Junior High band. The concert will be held at 7 p.m. on May 13 in the gym. A presentation of all three bands combined will conclude the program.

Short news items that are important enough to carry in a school newspaper but not long enough to warrant a separate story can be grouped together in one column with each story having a separate head, as illustrated in the above example from The Cougar Print, *Chaffin Jr. High, Fort Smith, Arkansas.*

36

Juvenile crime up 30%

by Edward Bell

Although we seem to see or hear more and more about crimes being committed around the Ft. Smith area, the number of crimes in the area has actually dropped in the past few years.

According to Corporal Robert Stevenson, Ft. Smith police communications relations officer, the reported offenses in this area decreased from 7610 in 1981 to 7423 in 1982. This was a 2% decrease in crimes overall.

"We're concerned about crimes being committed by juveniles because in the past year they have gone up over 30%," explained Stevenson.

One of the major reasons for the recent increase in juvenile crimes, according to Stevenson, is that young people are pressured with growing up and may commit crimes for attention. Another reason is that, unlike in past years, juveniles are pressured more for money and have to find ways to get it.

Those criminal acts that have decreased recently include: burglaries are down over 20%. One of the major reasons for the decrease is that the citizens are forming neighborhood watch patrols. This means when someone is gone, a neighbor will watch their house in case of burglaries.

He added that people in Ft. Smith could help to continue to decrease crime by learning self-defense techniques and when walking somewhere, go in a group and stay in safe places.

"Crimes against individuals are worst in highly populated places such as the downtown area, the north and eastsides, and are especially bad around the malls. The crimes against residences are all evenly spread about the city," concluded Stevenson.

An interview with an authoritative figure can be turned into an interesting news story, as indicated by the above article from The Cougar Print, Chaffin Junior High, Fort Smith, Arkansas. *Note the use of the large initial letter as a graphic device to attract the reader to the story.*

Taba Program Tested

THREE PILOT TEACHERS

"Taba? What's that?"

"Where have you been lately!? That's the new 7th grade social studies program!"

Taba is an outline of the entire 7th grade curriculum being tested at Irving by three social studies teachers: Mrs. Dianne Williams, Mrs. Pamela Shaddock and Mr. Neal Cross.

This program was named after its originator, Dr. Hilda Taba. Dr. Taba spent fifteen years of research working through the University of San Francisco. The purpose of the program is to teach the students how to think critically by forming opinions of world problems, and by learning how to work on their own. Taba is just recently being tried in various parts of the United States, and it can be applied to any area of school work. It is planned to be taught in grades one through eight.

TEACHERS ATTEND CLASSES

To teach Taba, the teachers have to attend special classes at which they are trained to use materials and learn teaching strategies to take students through a process of thinking.

Mrs. Williams, Mrs. Shaddock and Mr. Cross attend classes once a week at the Public School Administration Building, P.S.A.B. Their classes are instructed by Mr. Neal Hafenmeister. Mr. Hafenmeister was taught these skills at a summer workshop.

SEQUENCIAL PROGRAM

Taba is a program in which everything is done in sequence. Instead of making the students memorize facts, Taba lets the students compare and generalize. For example, if the classes are studying Egypt and the type of society that Egypt had, the students could compare the different and like aspects of modern and ancient Egyptian society. By comparing, the students can get general ideas about society and life in Egypt. This procedure is carried out step by step so the students can get a complete understanding of the subject.

STUDENT INVOLVEMENT

The program will not be in full swing for about a month, but when all of the materials arrive and are prepared, they will be placed in room 107 for student use. The students are now being introduced to his new way of teaching by being instructed in how to read maps, and to form hypothesis. . .

"The idea is to get the students involved," commented Mrs. Shaddock, "and to teach them different ways of thinking."

It is hoped that Taba will be a success and will be expanded to 8th grade in the future.

Curriculum changes should be reported in junior high newspapers. Some students may not find the articles too interesting but parents as well as students should be kept informed. The above article from the Irving News, *Irving Junior High School, Lincoln, Nebraska, presents a story on curriculum changes in an interesting way.*

Strike averted; tentative agreement reached

By Sharon Blake

A possible strike was averted when negotiators for District 4J teachers and the school board, after negotiating steadily for 14 hours, reached a tentative agreement at six o'clock this morning.

The final vote on the new contract will be taken by the teachers early next week.

Both sides have been mobilizing for a strike for several weeks.

The issues that were the hardest to negotiate were just cause dismissal, reduction in force and transfer.

The just cause issue was settled when agreement was reached to give three-year probationary teachers the benefit of an arbitrator while the provisions for first and second year teachers will be the same as before.

The reduction in force issue will now use seniority to some extent, although certification and needs of the district will be taken into consideration.

In the transfer issue, the deadline date was extended.

The maternity leave issue was thrown out as a bargaining tool.

The above example from The Scribe, Madison Junior High School, Eugene, Oregon, shows the advantages of a mimeographed newspaper over a printed one. The story on the strike had broken the same morning the paper was distributed. The element of timeliness cannot be overlooked.

Now you are ready to write your lead. Keep in mind that a writer becomes expert only through rewriting. Never be satisfied with the first product. Rewrite and rewrite again, if necessary, in order to achieve a polished story. Be sure to use active rather than passive voice. It is much better to say "John threw the ball"

Wednesday, February 17, 1971   WEST SIDE STORY

What's Happening in Our Classes

Biology Classes

Scenes of freshmen students hiding their eyes, have been numerous the past few weeks. Students of biology classes, taught by Miss Virginia Burmeister, have been studying flowering plants, and reproduction, and cell reproduction.

The classes dissected frozen frogs on January 26. Bonnie Weinberg, a student in the three-four biology class, stated her feelings after her class had dissected the frogs. "I felt a little queezy, but it wasn't as bad as I expected." Diane Goldstein, in the one-two class, felt this way about the dissecting. "I thought it was interesting because you could actually view the frogs live organs."

The classes also viewed the beating heart of a chicken embryo.

Speech I

An amusing and unique unit has held the interest of Mrs. Karen Suroff's Speech I classes. Improvisations were p r e s e n t e d over a two way phone system as the students learned to persuade their fellow s t u d e n t s to do specific things.

Two students in the class would participate at one time. One would be on the phone in a small, taping room and would listen for a dial tone and then dial any two num-

bers. Mrs. Suroff would then, after getting the dial tone, press the ring button. The student on the other phone, which was in the main room, would answer the phone and the conversation would start. A speaker is attached so that the rest of the class could listen on to the conversation. The two students were given a role to play and their dialogue was made up on the spot. Some examples of these situations given were: A Kidnapper calling the child's mother; a boy calling his mother for he had just wrecked the car; and, a salesman trying to convince a customer to buy his product.

Aspirin was once the product trying to be sold, but the customer kept saying that he did not want to buy any. Finally, after the argument had gone on for a while, the customer admitted he needed the aspirin for a headache that the salesman had given him.

Most everyone participated in this fun project that has helped lead the class into the next unit of voice.

Language Arts Class

Mrs. Ruby Lapin's Language Arts classes have a new perspective. They are sending away for foreign newspapers to study and compare.

Each student will be sending about a dollar, to cover postage and handling, to the Chamber of Commerce of any city in the world, such as Saigon or Moscow, in hope of receiving and English language newspaper from that city. The addresses come from a book compiled by Mrs. Hope Shackelford, who taught Mrs. Lapin a special course last year. The students are hoping that all the newspapers will be from the same day, so that it will allow for better comparisons. As of now none of Mrs. Lapin's three classes have set a date to send away for the papers, but it will be soon, since the newspapers take about a month to arrive.

Social Studies

The first millionaire student of West Ladue might be from Mr. Jeffery Kopolow's modules 10-11 project social studies class. The 23 students will be playing a simulated stock market until the end of the school year.

All students in the class picked occupations out of a hat. They ranged from a milkman to a doctor and will receive salaries each week. Each student was given ten thousand dollars to buy any stocks they wished on a particular list of stocks established by the class Each stock on the list is from the New York Stock Exchange. The students will be able to buy and sell as they wish during class time. The object of the game is to accumulate the most money at the end of the school year. The game accompanies a unit on economy, that the class is currently studying.

Many junior high schools fail to cover adequately news that occurs in the classroom even though this is the place where students spend 90 per cent of their time. The above example from **West Side Story,** *West Ladue Jr. High School, Ladue, Mo., is an excellent way to cover classroom news.*

than "The ball was thrown by John." It is more concise and more interesting.

Acorn Appreciation Day Promotes Hanley's Paper

As an additional effort to sell more *Acorn* subscriptions, Acorn Appreciation Day was held on Monday, Nov. 20.

The journalism class made green and brown paper acorns with various slogans written on them. All *Acorn* subscribers wore them. Paper oak trees were worn by members of *The Acorn* staff.

When asked, *Acorn* sponsor Mr. Donoho said, "Thirty more subscriptions were sold, bringing the total number to 400."

The total cost of publishing *The Acorn* comes to approximately 1600 dollars each year. Subscriptions pay part of this, the School Board underwrites the rest of the cost.

A "Why" lead is illustrated by the above news story from The Acorn, *Hanley Junior High School, University City, Missouri.*

After the lead has been written, it is time to write the body of the news story.

The purpose of the body of the news story is to explain and elaborate the lead and to add details not included in the lead.

In planning a news story, study your notes and eliminate all unnecessary material. Then arrange the notes you have left in the order of decreasing importance by making a sketchy paragraph-by-paragraph outline.

The lead should merge smoothly into the first paragraph of the body. Good transition can be accomplished either by including the next most important fact after the lead or by explaining in more detail one of the facts given in the lead.

Each paragraph should contain only one main idea. Remember the rule that no paragraph is to exceed 40 words. At the same time, however, avoid using a series of very short paragraphs. It is best to vary the paragraph length as much as possible.

Transition between paragraphs may be accomplished by: (1) repeating a key word in the previous paragraph; (2) using a synonym referring to a key word in the previous paragraph; (3) referring to any fact in the previous paragraph; or (4) using the adjectives *this* and *that,* and the pronouns *he, she,* and *it,* if they refer to something or someone in the previous paragraph.

Regardless of the transitional device used, all paragraphs should begin with an interesting fact and be written in simple words.

Be definite and specific, and use the active voice rather than the passive voice.

The most important thing to remember in writing news stories is to be brief but complete. Don't overstate the facts, but don't leave anything out if its omission might cause the reader to misinterpret the story.

Editorializing has no place in news stories. Staff opinions and congratulations belong on the editorial page. Opinion may be placed in news stories by using direct quotes from news sources. Be sure to balance quotes and giving both sides of the situation.

As in writing leads, you cannot expect to write a story once and be satisfied that it is the best you can do. Rewriting is essential to good reporting.

When you have written your news story, use the following checklist to determine if you have written it satisfactorily:

(1) Does the story contain all the important facts?

(2) Have all facts been checked carefully with authoritative persons?

(3) Are the essential facts of the story given in the lead, with the most important fact given in the opening phrase of the first sentence?

(4) Are all names spelled correctly and are all persons identified?

(5) Are the facts of the story arranged in order of decreasing importance? Is the story so written that it can be cut off after any paragraph and still give the reader the complete idea of the story? This is called writing the story in INVERTED PYRAMID order. Sometimes stories have to be cut to fit the space allotted in

a newspaper. If a story is written in inverted pyramid order the least important facts will be the ones cut.

(6) Have all dates been verified?

(7) Are all paragraphs short?

(8) Does the story have variety of sentence structure and paragraph length?

(9) Do successive sentences begin in different ways?

(10) Are the six W's and H relegated to the second and even third paragraph if there are too many for the first paragraph?

(11) Does each paragraph begin with a significant or interesting fact in interesting, specific words?

(12) Is the story written without editorial comment?

(13) Is the story concise? This is very important, since space is limited in a paper. Write and rewrite until you have eliminated all unnecessary words, but be careful not to change the true meaning of the story.

(14) Is the story written in the third person? The pronouns *you, I,* and *we* are not used in news stories.

(15) Is the writing style simple, clear, and direct? Avoid "talking down" to the reader, but make sure you write in terms the reader can understand.

(16) Is the story written interestingly?

(17) Is the story free of errors in grammar, punctuation, and spelling?

(18) Is the story free of errors in style?

(19) Have you written and rewritten the story until you are sure it is the best possible?

(20) Would you be willing to have the story appear under your name?

There are four basic types of news stories: (1) the single-feature news story; (2) the multiple-feature news story; (3) the action news story; and (4) the quote news story.

The *single-feature* news story begins with the most important fact in the first paragraph, with each succeeding paragraph having the next most important fact.

The *quote* story usually begins with a summary of the story in the first paragraph, followed by a quote in the second paragraph, summary in the third paragraph, quote in the fourth paragraph, and so on. This exact order need not be followed. The story may have two paragraphs of quotation and one of summary, or vice versa. This type of story is used mainly for writing interviews or speeches, which is covered in more detail in Chapter X.

The *action* story usually begins with a summary paragraph or paragraphs. Then the story is retold in more detail in succeeding paragraphs. Sports stories are normally written in this order. Sports writing is covered in Chapter IX.

The *multiple-feature* story is just what the name implies, a news story with more than one feature. In this form, the first paragraph gives these features in the order of their importance. Paragraph two gives the important details of feature one, paragraph three the important details of feature two, and so on. The last paragraphs give the least important details of the features.

To determine the type of story to be written and to make sure that all stories contain the necessary news qualities each school newspaper should organize a staff to see that the newspaper is published efficiently.

A typical staff organization would be as follows:

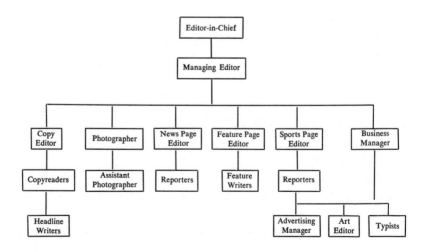

Staff organizations will vary depending upon the needs and the size of the staff. Duties of the staff members will also vary but in general the following would apply:

Editor-in-chief—Responsible for overall production of the paper. Along with the managing editor he should be responsible for writing editorials and laying out the editorial page. Some schools may prefer to have their own editorial page editor. The editor-in-chief should be responsible for reading all material including headlines and advertisements before it is sent to the printers.

Managing Editor—Responsible for seeing that all deadlines are met. Works cooperatively with the editor-in-chief in producing the editorial page. The managing editor should ok all copy before it is passed on to the editor-in-chief.

Copy Editor—Responsible for checking all copy for factual and grammatical errors. Also in charge of writing headlines.

News Page Editor—Assigns news stories to reporters. Makes sure they check their beats for possible stories. Responsible for makeup of the news page.

Feature Page Editor—Same as the news page editor except he is in charge of the feature page.

Sports Page Editor—Same as the news page editor except he is in charge of the sports page.

Photographer—Responsible for taking all pictures. Must follow instructions given him by the managing editor or page editors as to type of picture required. Must meet deadlines given to him by the editors.

Business Manager—In charge of the financial affairs of the newspaper. This includes the sale of subscriptions and advertising. In essence the business manager is the bookkeeper and is responsible for billing and crediting.

Art Editor—Responsible for doing all art work for the newspaper. The art editor normally is placed under the Business Manager because much of the art work for a school newspaper is found in advertising. However, the art editor is also responsible for editorial cartoons and other art work required by the editors.

Advertising Manager—Responsible for selling advertising. It

THE FOUR BASIC TYPES OF NEWS STORIES

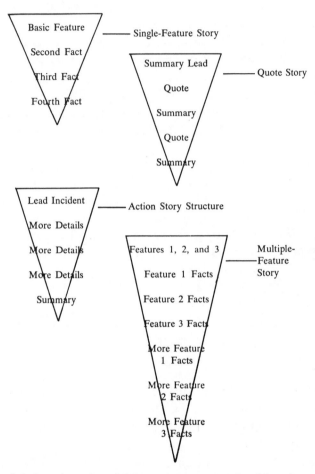

is essential that the advertising manager organize his salesmen so that all businesses in the community are called on.

Typists—Responsible for typing all stories before they are sent to the printers. They must meet deadlines given to them by the editors.

All staff members are reporters and all staff members should be assigned beats—regular places to check for stories. Reporters must get to know the people on their beats and they must keep their eyes and ears open for any news developments.

SINGLE-FEATURE STORY

Basic
Feature

Second Fact

Third Fact

Fourth Fact

Fifth Fact

Twenty-six of the 40 students from North who took their Science Fair exhibits to the Washington University Science Fair April 1–9 received either first, second, or third place in proficiency awards.

Danny Dolen, Kim Sears, John Doolittle, Sally Hutchings, and Bob Beam were the first-place winners.

Second-place awards went to Gary Bell, Bill Carr, John Lyons, John McNease, Cindy Nolan, Cathy Pender, Jason Kneis, Leslie Rolman, Janet Curry, Don Rope, and Elaine West.

Roger Bird, Toby Carr, Karen Hogan, Bob Leper, Mike Martin, Steve Soap, Pat Sartin, Debbie West, Jack Road, and Jim Toad received third-place awards.

Danny Dolan received $10 and the other first-place winners received $5. Second-place winners received $2 each.

MULTIPLE-FEATURE STORY

Features
1, 2, 3

Feature
1 Facts

Feature
2 Facts

Feature
3 Facts

More
Feature
1 and
Feature 3
Facts

Bleachers for the football fans, a change in the Constitution, and a bubble-gum-blowing contest were the subjects of discussion at last week's Student Council meeting.

An overflow of fans at this fall's football games brought about the need for additional bleachers. Bleachers now available seat only 200 people, and the average attendance at this year's games was 375.

Absentees from school will be able to vote in elections if the proposed change in the Constitution passes. The vote will take place on November 23.

A bubble-gum-blowing contest will be held on November 20 in order to raise money for the Student Council.

The estimated cost of the additional bleachers is $1,500. The bubble-gum-blowing contest is one of many activities planned in order to raise the money. The Student Council hopes to get the entire student body working on this project.

QUOTE STORY

Summary Lead

The Honorable Bill Bell, Missouri state representative from the 11th District, spoke to the fifth- and sixth-hour citizenship classes last Friday.

Representative Bell, a first-term representative, discussed government in general as he told the students about the duties of a state representative and the meaning of some of the current legislation.

Quote

"People in politics are getting younger every day," Representative Bell said. "One state representative is only 24 years old."

Summary

Students should take an interest in politics if our nation is to maintain its democratic ideals, according to Representative Bell.

Quote

He stated that he had gone into politics because "I felt, in my many years of associating with the government, there was a wall between government and farmers. I wanted to help break down that wall."

Summary

Representative Bell is interested in breaking down that wall because he also operates a farm near Bolivar, Mo., in his spare time.

The proposed bill to raise the driving age from 16 to 18 was discussed by Representative Bell.

Quote

"I don't think the county folk will ever go along with a bill to raise the driving age," he said.

Summary

Among other topics discussed by Representative Bell were reapportionment, capital punishment, and extending the governor's term of office.

ACTION STORY

Lead Incident
A tremendous fourth-quarter comeback fell short as North dropped its first basketball game of the year last Friday to Parkway South by a score of 42 to 38. A disastrous third quarter that saw North score only two points on a basket by Jim Jackson left the Ramblers behind 35 to 23.

More Details
Bill Jones hit a layup to start the fourth quarter, making the score 35 to 25. Parkway then scored five points, and North scored one on a free throw by Steve Hall. At this point Parkway enjoyed its biggest lead of the game, 40 to 26. North then started its comeback.

More Details
Free throws by Mathias, Paul Bisen, and Bill Jackson made the score 40 to 29. A layup by Jackson and a five-foot jump shot by Hall cut the margin to seven points.

More Details
A free throw by Parkway's John Amish made it 41 to 33, but a jump shot by Jackson under the basket cut the lead to six. Jackson was fouled on the shot and made the free throw to make the score 41 to 36.

More Details
North led only one time during the ball game, by a score of 19 to 18 with about two minutes left in the first half.

At the end of the first quarter North trailed 12 to 8 as they scored only one field goal.

More Details
Three straight baskets by Parkway's Jim McCarr and a 20-foot jump shot by Hall for the Ramblers gave Parkway an 18-to-10 lead early in the second quarter.

A free throw by Jackson, a tip-in by Jackson, and layups by Bisen and Hall gave North the lead.

More Details
Parkway quickly regained the lead 20 to 19 as John Tay scored on a driving layup. Two free throws by Parkway's Mike Marcin increased the Colts' lead to three. Jackson then scored on a fadeaway jump shot to end the first half with North trailing 22 to 21.

Summary
Then came the disastrous third quarter in which North scored only two points to the Colts' 13. Missed free-throw opportunities hurt North in this quarter as they did throughout the game.

EXERCISES

(1) Write leads from the following facts. Write leads only, not the entire story. At times, additional information has been given that need not be included in the lead.

    (a) Student Council officers elected John King, president
        Bill Benz, vice-president
        Lydia Ricardo, secretary
        Jack James, treasurer
        Wednesday, May 19, in homerooms
        Serve next school year
        Three candidates for each office

    (b) Ninth-Grade dance
        Friday, January 17, 8 P.M.
        Cafetorium
        School clothes
        Theme—"Winter Wonderland"
        "The Newsomes," a combo, will play
        Door prizes
        Tickets 25¢ each
        Dates not allowed

    (c) B. C. Burns replaces E. L. Adams as Principal
        Effective June 10
        E. L. Adams—principal for past nine years
        B. C. Burns—former assistant principal at Melbourne Jr.
          High in Kansas City
        E. L. Adams to become principal at the senior high

    (d) PTA Open House
        October 8, 7:30 P.M.
        Parents to visit all classes
        Teachers to tell aims and goals of class
        Refreshment period to follow
        Ten-minute classes
        All parents invited

    (e) Two ninth graders
        Charles Luncy and John Malin
        Exhibit art work
        St. Louis County Teacher's Art Club

Saturday, October 23

Students chosen on basis of work done in art this year

Students drew pictures at meeting

(f) Turkey-game tickets on sale next week

Ten North students selling

50¢ each

Student selling most to be given $10

Game against Nevada on November 24

(g) Chorus to give concert

97 ninth graders

Saturday, March 17

8 P.M. in auditorium

Public invited—free of charge

Patriotic music to be sung

(h) Poster contest on school spirit

Sponsored by Student Council

Entries due in two weeks

Winner to receive $5

Art teachers will judge

Posters to be displayed throughout school

(i) $1,000,000 bond issue

Passed by Avilla voters last Tuesday

6,314 to 2,100—needed two-thirds vote

To build two new elementary schools

Addition to North—eight rooms

All to be completed in two years' time

(j) Footlighters' dramatics presentation

The Neighbors—three-act drama

December 4–5 at 8 P.M. in auditorium

Jim Ruby and Ann Runyon in lead roles

Tickets 25¢ in advance, 35¢ at door

(2) Write news stories from the following facts:

(a) Martha Scott, eighth grader, wins poster contest on subject of school beautification.

Poster depicts ways students can help beautify school.

Martha has won several art awards including the Mayor's Art Award given by the city of Oronogo every year. She won this in 1967 as a seventh grader.

$10 award

70 students entered contest.

Poster to be reproduced and put on hall bulletin boards in every building.

(b) Faculty holds picnic

Saturday, September 17, Beloit Park

Volleyball—men against women

Women won 15 to 13

Led by Mrs. Joan Pounds, home economics teacher, who spiked the ball hard and served so well the men couldn't return it.

Purpose—so new teachers and old ones could get to know each other better.

45 members of the faculty attended, plus families.

(c) Latin Club

Sponsor—Mrs. Delores White

To attend banquet at Crestwood Junior High

November 13, 6:30 P.M.

Latin students to entertain Crestwood Latin students

Will present play *Victoria Satus*

Authors—Jane Ullman and Bob Henry, ninth graders

Bill Bruce, Jane Conley, Sarah Fisher, and Joe Blot to play lead roles

John Lewis and Mary Martin on committee to coordinate banquet

(d) Science club—Mrs. John Morris, sponsor

Field Trip—Beloit Park

Saturday, September 24

20 of 25 members attended

Study wildlife

Ended with picnic

Janice Leigh entertained by singing folk songs

Bill Bonn stung by a bee

Nancy Lee bitten by a bull snake—not poisonous

Jeff Newton fell down cliff and broke leg

Everyone mosquito-bitten

Mrs. Morris—"I think everyone had an exciting time, but I hope we don't have so many accidents on future field trips."

Bull snake now on display in classroom

Jeff will have leg in cast for six weeks but will return to school next week on crutches. He broke his leg following the picnic and was rushed to the hospital by Mrs. Morris.

(e) Citizenship students, sixth hour, Mr. Jim Bye, teacher
Study local government by participating as local officials
Jeff Benn—Mayor
Ronnie Neff, Jerry Heifman, Lorrie Astor, and Mary Cary —Councilmen
Tim Watt—Police Chief
Jerry Dan—Fire Chief
Larry Nees—City Attorney
Toni Block—City Judge
Bill Black, Bob Bolen, Dick Snyder, and Sandy Grote— Policemen
Lucy Lestor—City Clerk
Spent one day—January 12—Friday working alongside regular officials to see what job was like.
Firsthand knowledge gained, according to Mr. Bye.
Jeff—"I never knew the Mayor had so much work to do."
Tim—"We made only 10 arrests, but that was enough."
Jerry—"There were only three fire alarms during the day and they were all grass fires. In a way I'm glad there weren't any big fires, because we would probably only have been in the way. Still, it was quite exciting to ride on the fire truck."

(f) Good Conduct Week February 5–9
Sponsored by Student Council's code of conduct committee
Purpose: to instill pride in the student body
February 5 will be cleanup day—pick up trash on school grounds
February 6 will be good-grooming day—boys wear coats and ties and girls good school clothes
February 7 will be keep-cafeteria-clean day
February 8 students will help teachers clean rooms
February 9 will be an essay contest on good conduct to be submitted to Student Council
Rules for contest: No Student Council member may enter
200–300 words in length

typewritten on one side of page
Prizes for contest: $10 for first place
$5 for second place

(g) New Student Council officers elected
Tom Scott—president
George Lindley—vice president
Sarah Bopp—secretary
Jill Abbey—treasurer
Tom is the first eighth-grade president in the history of the school. President is normally from ninth grade.
Each student participates in many school activities. (Use names of school organizations to fill in here.)
Tom plans to have Council sponsor a foreign child and raise money to buy a new scoreboard for basketball. He also wants a faculty talent show and a school motto adopted.

(h) "The Swinging Five" to play at ninth-grade dance
Theme of dance—"Winter Wonderland"
Date—December 9
Planning Committee—Steve Logan, Ashley Drake, Lynlea Corey, Betty Brand
Time: 8–10
Place: School gym
Dress: coat and tie for boys and good school clothes for girls
Next dance to be February 8
Two eighth graders in "The Swinging Five"—Joe Blake, Richard Day; others in senior high
Admission: 35 cents
Decoration Committee—Debby Straut, Carol Keys, Robert Morgan, Becky Tate, Jack Jabos
Ninth-grade class sponsor: Mr. George Hailey
No dates allowed

(i) Core class takes up collection to sponsor foreign child
Ten-year-old boy in Viet Nam
Mrs. Virginia Hall's first- and second-hour core class
Bob James' idea
Each member of class to give 25 cents each month for support
Class study of Viet Nam stimulated idea

Letters from child posted on bulletin board outside office
Name of child: Tien Ling
Class will send Christmas present
Donations acceptable
Clothes and toys needed
Must have by November 30 to reach Viet Nam by Christmas

(j) Ninth-grade play tryouts
Wednesday, January 9
Production to be March 2–3
Name of play—*Little Women*
Sponsor—Mr. Bill Valenti, speech teacher
Student director—Vicky Jones
3:15 in school auditorium
Parts for seven girls and four boys
Backstage personnel also needed—any interested student see Mr. Valenti

(3) Divide the class into three teams. Have one team watch the ABC evening news, one watch the NBC evening news, and one watch the CBS evening news. Have team members compare notes and then report to the class on whether or not the network presented its news in a balanced and objective manner. Discuss what story each network used as its lead stories and what stories were covered by one network but not by the others.

(4) Rewrite the leads of five news stories in a recent issue of your school newspaper. Be prepared to discuss any changes you made in class.

(5) Clip five stories from your local newspaper and write a short paper on each describing how they meet the five qualities of news stories.

(6) Write 25 sentences, at least 10 words in length, in which you use active voice.

(7) Clip five news stories from a newspaper. Cut each story apart by paragraphs and put each story in a separate envelope. In class, exchange your envelopes with another student and see if each one can put the stories back in the same order as they appeared in the newspaper. Be sure to write down the first couple of words of each paragraph before you cut the stories apart in order to verify the correct order.

Chapter IV

WRITING EYE-CATCHING HEADLINES

Headline writing—to many the most difficult part of journalism —may be the most challenging part for some. Many talented journalistic writers have a difficult time capping their story with a headline that attracts. Just as a male or a female with an attractive head captures the interest of others, so will an interesting headline catch the reader's eye.

For every story assigned a reporter to write, there should be a reason behind the assignment. Whatever that reason is should be the essence of what the headline is about.

Remembering why a story was written should make headline writing easy—not difficult. If reporters know what the basic idea is that they have developed their story around, they should then realize that it is that same idea that should be captured in the headline.

It is impossible to tell the reader the complete story in a headline. In some cases, this might mean summarizing a 500-word story in 8 to 10 words. News story heads should summarize the story as much as possible, but heads for feature stories should point out the outstanding facts or characteristics that are worth knowing, regardless of what the story is about.

Condensing the first sentence of a story and setting it in headline form will not necessarily capture the reader.

Imagination can be used in writing headlines but writers should not get "cute" by referring to some obscure part of the story that does not center around the reason the story was written in the first place.

Headlines should come from the color, the emotion, and the impact of the story. Then, and only then, will headline writers be counting readers instead of characters.

Character count is an important aspect of headline writing, as all heads must fit the space allotted to them. Headlines that are too long may extend into the column divider or above another story. A headline that is too short may trap white space in the middle of a page, which is unattractive to the eye. White space can help a page look more attractive but it generally does not when the white space occurs because a headline is too short.

Although there is no set rule for the minimum length of a head, a good guideline to follow would be to write all heads so that they are no more than two counts under the maximum. Thus, a headline that has a maximum count of 24 would have a minimum count of 22. Fitting headlines this way generally shows that real effort has been made for writing the best headline possible.

Character counts for headlines may vary according to the printer's schedule. In general, the following character counts are customary:

Capital M & W—2 counts
Capital I—1 count
All other capitals—1½ count
Lower case m and w—1½ count
Lower case f, l, i, t—½ count
All other lower case letters—1 count
Space between words—1 count
Commas, semicolons, colons, single quote marks, hyphens—½ count
Numerals—1 count
Question mark, dollar sign, percent sign—1 count
Symbol for and (&)—1 count (Should be used only if part of an official title)

Headlines are counted by the line. Do not count both lines of a two-line headline together. Figure the count for the following headline:

Ancient History Class

Visits Prehistoric Pit

If you got 20 for the top line and 19½ for the bottom line you are correct.

There are several methods of counting headlines. A writer should choose the one he works with best and use it all the time to insure accuracy. Regardless of the method used, all headlines should be counted twice. If the same answer is reached both times the writer can be relatively certain that his answer is correct. However, if a different character count is arrived at the second time, then a third or maybe even fourth count is necessary. Remember, headlines are designed for eye appeal and to capture the essence of the story. A poorly counted headline takes away from the attractiveness of an entire page.

A common method used by many head writers for counting heads is simply to count each word separately and place the character count after each word. Then add together the total count remembering to include the count for spaces between each word. The example below shows that by adding the count of each word, the count is 27½ plus two for spaces between words, which makes the total character count 29½.

Letters Commend Twenty-Three

By adding $6½ + 8½ + 12½ + 2$ the total of 29½ is reached. This method of counting generally speeds up the counting process. If the headline is too short or too long it is generally possible to substitute for only one word and make the head fit. This saves counting all the words over again.

Counting headlines is really simple mathematics. However, it can become confusing working with fractions. It might be easier to pair fractions to count.

Officers Price, Rice Give Legal Counseling

In the above head fractions might be paired like this:

Letters	Total Count
Of	2 (1½ + ½)
fi	3 (½ + ½)
cers	4, 5, 6, 7
Space	8
Pi	9, 10 (1½ + ½—pairing the i in Price with the P)
rce	11, 12, 13
,R	14, 15 (½ + 1½)
Space	16
ii	17 (½ + ½—pairing the i in Rice with the i in Give)
ce	18, 19
Space	20
Gl	21, 22 (1½ + ½—pairing the G in Give with the l in legal)
ve	23, 24
Space	25
Ll	26, 27 (1½ + ½—pairing the L in legal with the l in counseling)
ega	28, 29, 30
Space	31
Ci	32, 33 (1½ + ½—pairing the C and i in counseling)
ounseng	34, 35, 36, 37, 38, 39, 40

The above way can be confusing, as it means looking ahead to find fractions for pairing and then remembering to include in the count the characters skipped over. However, for some writers it can assure accurate counting.

Another way to count headlines is to first count the whole units above the line, then do the half units below the line, and then total the two together. For example:

To avoid fractions altogether it is possible to count all ½ units on the bottom as shown above as one and then divide by two. This way you would not have to add fractions.

Accuracy in counting headlines is much more important than speed. At deadline time, however, speed will sometimes be essential, so each writer should use the method he can best adapt to for speed and accuracy.

Counting headlines is actually a secondary step in the head-line-writing process. The first step is to write a good, attractive headline that fits the space. To write a headline that will assure reader appeal, it is important to follow a few rules.

It is essential that an outstanding fact be placed in the top line of a head. When writing a two-line head, it is best to place the subject and verb on the top line and the preposition and object on the bottom line, as shown in the following example:

It is not always possible to write heads this way. Sometimes the subject may be too long to place the verb on the same line, so the verb may be placed on the bottom line as in the following example:

Subject
/

Wage, hour laws cover teenagers

╱
Verb

However, *the preposition and its object should not be separated.* The following examples show how it should *not* be done. The preposition "to" should be on the same line as its object "Cape" and the preposition "At" should be on the same line as its object, "Festival."

The following headlines have also split the preposition from its object. What is the preposition in each headline and what is its object?

1 **concert basis for
ecological theme**

2 **The Lord Works In
Beautiful Ways**

3 *Student Voices Concern Over Racial
Situation in Local Educational System*

4 *Study Halls Possible If
Student Center Is Built*

In number 1 above, the preposition is "for" and the object is "theme." "In" is the preposition in the second headline and its object is "Ways." There are two prepositions in number 3, but only one is split from its object. That one is "over" and its object is "situation." In number 4 the object "center" is split from its preposition, "if."

Parts of the same verb should also be kept together on the same line. In the following examples the verbs "Have Begun" and "May Be Organized" have been split.

Intramurals Have
Begun
League May
Be Organized

The noun and its adjacent adjective should be kept together on the same line. In the following example the noun is "policy" and its adjective is "Attendance." They should not be separated as the example shows.

Attendance
policy changes
at North

If possible, *the verb and its object should also be on the same line.* However, most copy editors will accept a headline if the verb and object are split. Headline writers, though, should never be satisfied with less than the best. In the following example the verb is "Plans" and it has two objects, "Concerts" and "Center."

Council of Youth Plans
Concerts, Youth Center

It is also important that *first and last names of a person be kept together on the same line.* If the first name is not used, then initials should be used, unless the individual is well known and there can be no doubt about what person the headline is referring to. In most schools, there are many people with the same last name, so it is usually best to use first name or first two initials of a person if possible for clear identification.

There should be a verb expressed or implied in all heads and each head should have a subject. The first two heads below have no subjects and the third one has no verb. Thus, all three heads fail to feature the complete idea behind the story.

1. ## Check into Mental Health

2. ## Offers 14 Courses

3. ## *Junior Achievement*

Forms of the verb "to be" should be omitted in headlines, as they are generally passive in nature. The verb "to be" may be used, however, to indicate future tense. A newspaper staff should decide whether they are going to use "to be" or "will be" for future tense and stick to one or the other for consistency. The verbs "is," "are," "was," and "were" should not be used in headlines. Generally they are space fillers and serve no useful purpose. The verbs "is" and "are" can be understood verbs in headlines; however, they are often passive and should be avoided. The following head could have been written, "Volleyball First." The word "is" is simply a space filler.

Volleyball is first

Verbs should be written in the active voice rather than the passive. In other words, the subject should be doing the action. The following headlines are all passive as indicated by the "-ed" verbs.

49 honored by WMA honor society assembly

Meeting Planned For Teachers

35 Seniors commended

The headlines could have been rewritten in the active voice. For example:

> WMA Honors 49
> Teachers Plan Meeting
> Principal Commends 35 Seniors

Each of the revised headlines has been rewritten so that the subject is doing the action. The WMA honors, the teachers plan, and the principal commends.

Only present and future tenses are used in headlines. The passive voice almost always tends to imply past tense. In the three above headlines the verbs "is" or "are" could be understood in each one, making the headlines present tense, but that does not eliminate the passive voice. Present tense is used for both present and past stories, and future tense for future stories.

Numbers may be used in headlines in Arabic form unless they begin a line, in which case they should be written out. This is particularly true of the first line of a headline; headlines are written like sentences, and sentences should not begin with a numeral. The following headlines should have their numerals spelled out.

3 Come To Learn English

6 Achieve Merit Rating

3 AFS students experience new school

Only well-known abbreviations are used in a headline, and abbreviations are used without periods in most cases. The following headlines should not have periods after their abbreviations, and it is doubtful that most readers would know what E.E.E. is or what I.S. is. Most schools, however, do give the P.S.A.T. test and many have a D.E.C.A. chapter, so those abbreviations are more readily understood. P.E. is a common abbreviation for physical education. However, remember that abbreviations should not be followed by periods.

D.E.C.A. reaches for the top

Parkway offers E.E.E.

I. S. begins a new year

P.E. Adds Coed Classes

P.S.A.T. test to be given October 22

The words "a," "an," and "the," are space fillers in most cases and should not be used. If they are part of a title, it is satisfactory to use them. The word "a" in the following headline could have been eliminated without changing the meaning of the head. Don't use "a," "an," or "the" just to enable the character count to fit.

A Frustrated Lot Speaks Out

The word "and" is also a space filler. A comma could have been used to substitute for it in the following heads.

New Teachers, Less Smoking and Demerits Start Off 74-75 Year

Teachers and students switch clothes for a day

Bicycle And Car Equal Confusion

Majorettes and Poms Do Their Own Thing

When quotations are used in heads, single quote marks, rather than double, are usually used, to save space. The following head has used double quote marks.

"You haven't seen nothing yet"

Headlines are not to be written as announcements as in the following examples

Here They Are: Queen Candidates

Other headline rules that should be followed include:

(1) Do not editorialize except in editorial heads.

(2) Do not abbreviate days and months unless specific date is given. For example "January" by itself should be spelled out, but it is satisfactory to write "Jan. 17."

(3) Do not repeat key words in a head or forms of the same word.

(4) Do not begin a headline with a verb.

(5) Use Miss, Mrs., Ms. or Mr. for adults.

(6) Use strong verbs, forceful and dynamic. All headline